D1178744

Ripley's

Believe It or Not!®

Sports Oddities

SCHOLASTIC BOOK SERVICES
New York Toronto London Auckland Sydney Tokyo

 This edition is published by Scholastic Book Services, a division of Scholastic Magazines, Inc., by arrangement with Ripley Enterprises, Inc.

5th printing......April 1974

Printed in the U.S.A.

THE "ODDS" IN SPORTS

A Preface by Max Kase, Sports Columnist

Interested in sports oddities? There's a gold mine of fantastic achievements and incredible accomplishments in the bulging files of the "Ripley's Believe It or Not." This feature was started by Bob Ripley back in 1918, and researchers, down through the years, have dredged up a treasure trove of unusual happenings with the record books authenticating the findings.

For instance, there was a football game of rugby played by the Matani of West Africa using a human head for a ball . . . Tom McAuliffe of Buffalo, an armless golfer, played 18 holes in 98 strokes . . . J. Darby of England jumped backward 12 feet, 11 inches and to make it tougher, he did it with weights . . . Ol' Battling Levinsky, who once fought three times in one day, had a record of around 400 bouts but he didn't compare to a guy named Commodus, who fought 1,031 battles (161-192) and was so proud of his records in the gladiatorial arena that he commanded the world to worship him as Hercules. How did he come to his end? At the hands of a wrestler by the name of Narcissus, who strangled him!

And there are many, many more sports oddities that you will enjoy in this book.

The first "Believe It or Not" cartoon, published in the *New York Globe*, December 19, 1918.

The biggest track meet in baseball history occurred on August 25, 1922. In the wildest-scoring, wildest-hitting nine-inning game on record, the Cubs beat the Phillies 26-23 after both teams had banged out a total of 51 hits.

KOO-TAH-WE-COTS-OO-LEL-E-HOO-LA-SHAR
a Pawnee Indian
CLOCKED BY AMERICAN ARMY OFFICERS
WITH STOP WATCHES, RAN THE MILE IN
3 MINUTES, 58 SECONDS IN 1876
MODERN RUNNERS NEVER EQUALLED
THAT RECORD UNTIL 1954

Johann SCHRAUDOLPH
of Einodsbach, Germany
AT THE AGE OF 10 BECAME THE FIRST PERSON TO CLIMB MT. MADELEGABEL- 8,680 FEET HIGH -
AND REPEATED HIS FEAT 7 TIMES EACH YEAR UNTIL HE REACHED THE AGE OF 71

CHARLES BOSWELL BLIND GOLFER of Birmingham, Ala. SHOT AN 81 -YET HE HAD NEVER PLAYED GOLF UNTIL AFTER HE WAS BLINDED BY SHELLFIRE IN WORLD WAR II

ROGER ZUBARIK
of Goldsboro, N.C.,
PLAYING FOOTBALL WITH THE
Little League Green Bay Packers
SCORED 2 TOUCHDOWNS IN THE FIRST 26 SECONDS OF A GAME (Dec.8, 1962)

No sporting event in history has ever matched the two Dempsey-Tunney fights for attendance and gate receipts. Their first bout (September 23, 1926) drew 120,757 fans who paid $1,895,733 at the gate. Their second fight (September 22, 1927) drew 104,943 fans who paid $2,658,660. Tunney's share of the latter purse was $990,000—or $33,000 for each minute of fighting!

EDDIE
ARCARO
RIDING IN 6 RACES
ON JUNE 7, 1957
Belmont Race Track
FINISHED
1ST
2D
3D
4TH
5TH
AND
6TH!

8 GREYHOUNDS CROSSED THE FINISH LINE
IN THE SAME ORDER AS THEIR POST POSITIONS!
7th Race, Jacksonville (Fla.) Kennel Club - Jan. 23, 1950

3 CYCLISTS from India
- ADI B. HAKIM, JAL P. BAPASOLA, AND RUSTOM J. BHUMGARA-
CIRCLED THE WORLD IN A PERIOD OF 4 YEARS, 5 MONTHS, 3 DAYS
COVERING
44,000 MILES
(Oct. 15, 1923 - March 18, 1928)

THE MOST STRENUOUS RACE IN HISTORY

GIPSY MOTH III, A YACHT WEIGHING 13 TONS, AND 39 FEET, 7 INCHES LONG, WHICH NORMALLY REQUIRES A CREW OF 6 MEN, WON A RACE FROM PLYMOUTH, ENGLAND, TO NEW YORK WITH ONLY FRANCIS CHARLES CHICHESTER, AGED 59, ABOARD—

CHICHESTER, RACING FOUR OTHER YACHTS EACH MANNED BY A SINGLE SAILOR, COVERED 4,000 MILES IN 40½ DAYS (June 11 to July 21, 1960)

THE LONGEST WRESTLING MATCH—
ALF DAVEY—OF ENGLAND WRESTLED JOHN SHEA
11½ HOURS BEFORE A FALL (MICHIGAN—1908)

Golfdom's only grand slam was accomplished by an *amateur*—Bobby Jones. At age 28 in 1930 he captured the British Open, British Amateur, U.S. Open, and U.S. Amateur tournaments. In the most grueling of all tests, the U.S. Open, the baby-faced Atlantan achieved this phenomenal feat between 1923 and 1930—4 victories, 2 ties for first, and 1 second.

OSWALD
FOHN
of Lauerz,
Switzerland
THREW A
BOULDER
WEIGHING
183 POUNDS
A DISTANCE
OF 9 FEET,
5 INCHES
1955

WILLIAM
BOLTON
of Harewood, England
HIKED
400 MILES
FOR EXERCISE
10 TIMES EACH
YEAR FOR THE
LAST 10 YEARS OF HIS LIFE
-UNTIL HIS DEATH
AT THE AGE OF 80

THE PARATROOPER WHO JUMPED UP!

LT. ROBERT FARRIS
of Fort Rucker, Ala.,
JUMPING FROM A PLANE AT 2,500 FEET,
**WAS CARRIED IN AN UPDRAFT
TO A HEIGHT OF 3,000 FEET**
***- AND TOOK 24 MINUTES TO
REACH THE GROUND***

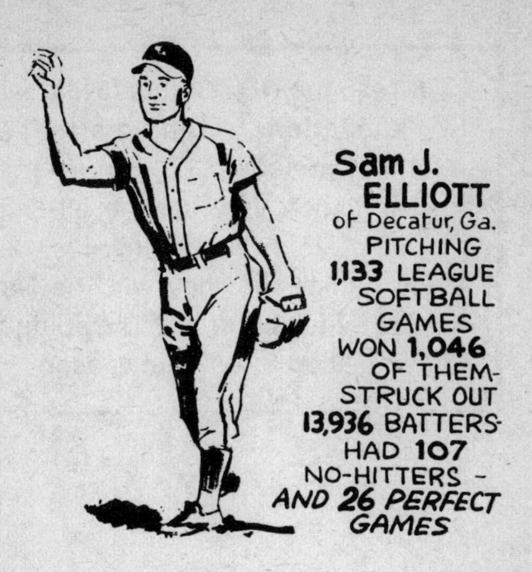
Sam J. ELLIOTT
of Decatur, Ga.
PITCHING
1,133 LEAGUE SOFTBALL GAMES
WON 1,046 OF THEM-
STRUCK OUT 13,936 BATTERS-
HAD 107 NO-HITTERS -
AND 26 PERFECT GAMES

"MERRICK"
an American race horse that died in 1941
HAD THE LONGEST LIFE OF ANY REGISTERED HORSE - 38 YEARS
IT WON 61 RACES AND FINISHED SECOND 40 TIMES IN 205 RACES

In 1916 the N.Y. Giants fashioned two sensational winning streaks. First they reeled off 17 victories in a row and then they set the all-time record of 26 straight wins. By how many games did they win the National League pennant? They didn't. They finished *fourth* that season!

DICK
FOWLER
- ATHLETICS -
PITCHED A
NO-HIT-NO-RUN
GAME
IN HIS FIRST
BIG LEAGUE
GAME

JACK TERRY CROSSED THE ENGLISH CHANNEL FROM DOVER TO CALAIS

ON A TRICYCLE

HE MADE THE TRIP IN 8 HOURS, KEPT AFLOAT BY THE RUBBER TIRES AND STEERING WITH HIS REAR WHEEL

July 28, 1883

The greatest goose-egg collector of all time was Grover Cleveland Alexander. Pitching for the Phillies in 1916, Alex hurled 33 victories, of which 16 were shut-outs.

40
STRIKEOUTS
IN ONE GAME
LEFTY
GOMEZ
FANNED 22 MEN
IN 9 INNINGS
BUT LOST!
HIS OPPONENT, A. Soares.
FANNED 18
Craft Club
vs
Point Reyes
California

"PEANUTS"
BARBETTA
Amateur Boxer-Corona, N.Y.
DEFEATED 27 TITLE-HOLDERS
BUT NEVER WON A TITLE HIMSELF

A high school team chalked up the greatest winning streak in basketball history. The Passaic (New Jersey) High School "Wonder Five" reeled off 159 victories in a row between 1920 and 1925.

LOUIS CYR
-Famous Canadian Strongman
LIFTED 545 POUNDS
WITH ONE FINGER

MISS "JACKIE" MITCHELL
FIRST LADY TO SIGN A PROFESSIONAL BASEBALL CONTRACT
ENGAGED BY CHATTANOOGA
MISS MITCHELL STRUCK OUT BABE RUTH AND LOU GEHRIG IN SUCCESSION IN AN EXHIBITION GAME
APRIL, 1931

BERT RECHICHAR
halfback for
the Baltimore Colts
KICKED A FIELD GOAL
OF **56** YARDS
-A WORLD'S RECORD-
ON HIS FIRST TRY
IN A PRO FOOTBALL
GAME
Sept. 27, 1953

CONRAD WILD
of Milwaukee, Wis.
ATTEMPTING TO
SHOW A BOWLING
INSTRUCTOR THE
HOOK THAT HAD
"RUINED" HIS
GAME, ROLLED
12 STRIKES IN
SUCCESSION
FOR HIS
FIRST 300
GAME

MRS. IVA JARVIS
of Phillipsburg, Kans.
FIRING EACH TIME
AT 2 CLAY PIGEONS
RELEASED
SIMULTANEOUSLY
SCORED 99
OUT OF A
POSSIBLE
100

DAVID QUINN
of Nederland, Texas
BOWLING ONLY 3 MONTHS
SCORED A PERFECT 300 GAME
IN AN ABC LEAGUE TOURNAMENT

LOUIS
"BUCK" NEWSOM
of the St. Louis Browns
PITCHING IN BOTH GAMES
OF A DOUBLE-HEADER
WALKED THE FIRST 4 MEN
IN ONE GAME AND THEN
STARTED THE SECOND GAME BY
STRIKING OUT THE SAME 4 PLAYERS!

The greatest woman athlete of all time, Babe Didrikson, entered 634 amateur contests in track, swimming, basketball, and billiards, and won 632 times. Upon taking up golf in her later years, she won 16 straight tournaments—a record that still stands.

THE MAN WHO DUELED WITH A FAN!

YASHITZONE

GREATEST DUELIST IN JAPANESE HISTORY

NEVER WORE EITHER HELMET OR ARMOR AND USED HIS SWORD ONLY FOR THE FINAL DEATH THRUST

-BEWILDERING HIS ARMORED OPPONENTS THROUGHOUT EACH DUEL BY FEINTS WITH A FAN!

ED
DELAHANTY
THE ONLY
PLAYER
WHO EVER
LED
BOTH THE
NATIONAL
AND
AMERICAN
LEAGUES
IN BATTING
.408-PHILADELPHIA(N.L.)1899
.376-WASHINGTON(A.L.)1902
HE WAS ONE OF
5 BROTHERS PLAYING
IN THE MAJOR LEAGUES
SIMULTANEOUSLY
P

THE BROOKLYN DODGERS
IN 3 CONSECUTIVE GAMES
PLAYED A TOTAL OF
56 INNINGS
May, 1920

The most successful pitching debut in history was recorded by Walter Johnson. In his first four days in the major leagues, the Senators' "Big Train" pitched all three games of a series against the Yankees—and shut them out each time, allowing a total of only 12 hits!

JIMMY
NICHOLS
ONE-ARM
GOLFING STAR
MADE A
336-YARD
HOLE-IN
ONE
Douglas,
Georgia
1933
ALTHOUGH LEFT-HANDED -
HE USES A RIGHT-HAND STANCE

THE UNIVERSITY OF MIAMI
DID NOT COMPLETE A SINGLE PASS IN THE 1946 ORANGE BOWL GAME
-YET ITS WINNING TOUCHDOWN WAS SCORED ON A PASS
AL HUDSON INTERCEPTED A PASS AFTER THE PLAYING TIME HAD OFFICIALLY EXPIRED AND RAN 89 YARDS FOR A GOAL

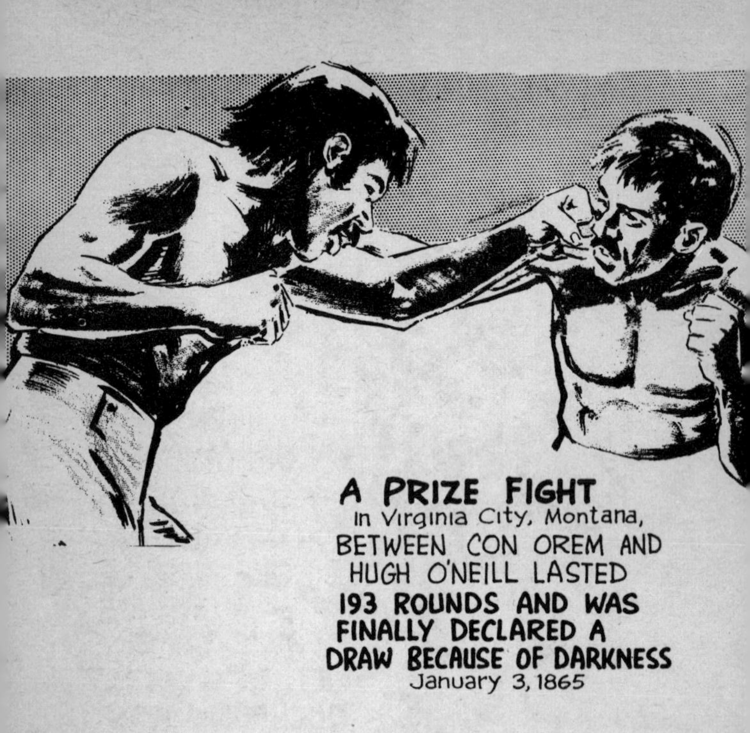

In the fifth inning of a game against the Red Sox on June 9, 1908, the Indians recorded a feat that had never been done before or has been equalled since—every Indian got up to bat, made a hit, and scored a run.

C
NEAL
BALL
MADE AN
UNASSISTED
TRIPLE PLAY
AND A
HOME RUN
IN THE
SAME
INNING
Cleveland
July 19,
1909

George
WEGENER
AGE 14
PORTAL, N.D.
SCORED A
HOLE-IN-ONE
FROM ONE
COUNTRY
TO ANOTHER
HE DROVE ACROSS THE
BORDER FROM THE 9TH TEE IN CANADA
AND INTO THE CUP ON THE 9TH GREEN IN UNITED STATES
Gateway Golf Club – U.S. and Canada

HARRY HULEN
of Minneapolis
WAS AT BAT
6 TIMES
WALKED
6 TIMES
AND SCORED
6 TIMES
Aug. 1, 1894

THE LOS ANGELES ANGELS
Pacific Coast League baseball team
COMPLETED DOUBLE PLAYS
IN 6 CONSECUTIVE INNINGS
Sept. 25, 1934

THE LONGEST HOLE-IN-ONE IN HISTORY
LOU KRETLOW of Edmond, Okla.,
PLAYING THE PAR 4 16TH HOLE OF THE LAKE HEFNER GOLF COURSE AT OKLAHOMA CITY,
MADE A 427-YARD HOLE-IN-ONE

Between August 2, 1931, and August 3, 1933, the Yankees never stopped "running." During this period of just over two years, the Bronx Bombers played 308 games without suffering a shut-out.

ALVIN H. GETZ of San Francisco, Calif.
PLAYING TABLE TENNIS AGAINST HIMSELF
COMPLETED 2,000 VOLLEYS WITHOUT A MISS

JOHN G.
GUILFORD
of Palatka, Fla.,
BOWLED 9
SUCCESSIVE
STRIKES
-YET HE IS
TOTALLY
BLIND!

The only major league game in which *nobody* got a hit in nine innings was played on May 2, 1917. Fred Toney was pitching for the Reds and Jimmy Vaughan for the Cubs. In the top of the 10th, Toney "fell apart" and was reached for two hits and a run.

On May 15, 1941, Joe DiMaggio belted out a couple of hits—and he kept banging out at least one safety a game until July 17. All in all, Jolting Joe collected 91 hits off 73 pitchers in 56 straight games. Of his 91 safeties, 16 went for doubles, 4 for triples, and 15 for homers.

ELMER SMITH
of the Cleveland Indians
MADE 7 CONSECUTIVE
EXTRA-BASE HITS
—TOTALING
22 BASES
4 HOMERS
3 DOUBLES
1921

THE MAN WHO CROSSED THE ATLANTIC WITHOUT FOOD OR WATER!

DR. ALAIN BOMBARD a Frenchman, SAILED A SMALL RAFT FROM THE CANARIES TO BARBADOS - A VOYAGE OF 65 DAYS - *EXISTING ON SEA WATER AND FISH HE CAUGHT ON THE TRIP!* 1953

"CHUCK"
DYKE
MAYOR OF BOYSTOWN
Cleveland, Ohio
FANNED 25 BATTERS
IN 9 INNINGS
AND MADE THE OTHER 2 PUTOUT THROWS
American Legion Baseball League

TONY FREITAS
-PITCHING FOR
SACRAMENTO, CALIF.,
STRUCK OUT A
BATTER AND
CAUGHT
THE
THIRD
STRIKE
THE BALL HIT THE
CATCHERS CHEST
PROTECTOR AND
BOUNCED TO
THE PITCHER'S BOX

In 1902 Michigan went west to swamp Stanford 49-0 in the first Rose Bowl football game. The Wolverines didn't return to the Rose Bowl for 46 years. Upon their return in 1948, they won by the same score, 49-0.

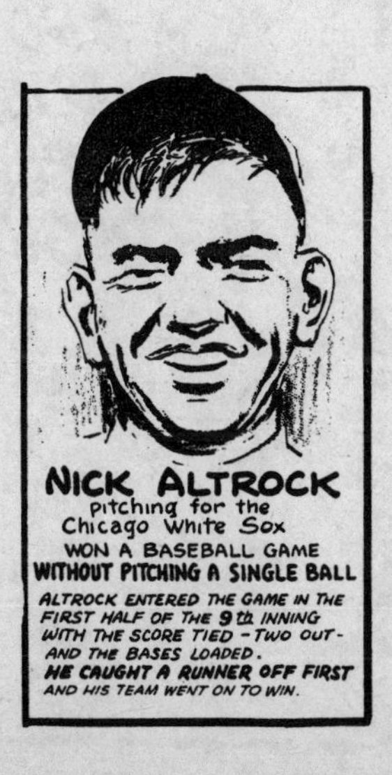

BABE
HERMAN
DOUBLED
WITH THE
BASES
FULL
AND A
DOUBLE
PLAY
RESULTED
HE
OVER-RAN
THE 2
BASERUNNERS
AHEAD
OF HIM

How many ways can a batter reach first base without hitting the ball?

(Answer, next page.)

A BATTER CAN REACH FIRST 6 WAYS WITHOUT HITTING THE BALL

Base on balls
Hit by pitched ball
Catcher missing 3rd strike
Substitute runner
Catcher interference
Catcher tipping bat

COUNTESS de POLIGNAC AND THE MARQUISE de NESLE
2 FRENCH NOBLEWOMEN, IN A DISPUTE OVER THE AFFECTIONS OF THE DUKE de RICHELIEU
FOUGHT A PISTOL DUEL AT 25 PACES—
MADAME de NESLE WAS WOUNDED IN THE SHOULDER
Paris, France - Sept. 10, 1718

TITA PIAZ (1879-1948)
famed Alpine guide of Cortina, Italy
CLIMBED THE FORBIDDING WINKLER TOWER
- 9,000 FEET OF SHEER ROCK -
WITH HIS 5-YEAR-OLD SON STRAPPED TO HIS BACK!
PIAZ- WHO HAD CLIMBED STEEP VAJOLET TOWER
300 TIMES WITHOUT A MISHAP-
DIED IN A FALL FROM A BICYCLE

DAVE KAISER

FORMER MICHIGAN STATE UNIVERSITY FOOTBALL STAR, KICKED ONLY **2** FIELD GOALS IN HIS ENTIRE GRID CAREER – INCLUDING BOTH HIGH SCHOOL AND COLLEGE COMPETITION – ***YET BOTH THOSE FIELD GOALS WON BOWL GAMES***

THE FIRST WON THE 1956 ROSE BOWL GAME FOR MICHIGAN, **17-14** – AND THE SECOND CLINCHED THE 1957 NORTH-SOUTH SHRINE GAME, **23-20**

First batter triples on first pitched ball. Pitcher takes position in box to pitch to second batter, runner on third decides to steal home, pitcher steps from box and throws home. Batter interferes with throw. Therefore the batter is out, and the runner goes back to third.

The next two batters go out the same way. This is repeated for the entire nine innings, and only one ball is pitched each inning.

Technically this is possible, but of course highly improbable.

If the Yankees had been paid for overtime in 1906, they would have wound up the season rich. They played a double-header every day for five straight days (August 30 through September 4)—and won all ten games!

TOM
HUGHES
PITCHED
NO-HIT
NO-RUN
GAMES
IN BOTH
THE
NATIONAL
AND
AMERICAN
LEAGUES
for New York
against Cleveland
1910
for Boston
against Pittsburgh
1916

WILLIE REINBOLD
of Naples on the Gulf, Florida
IN A 32-MILE CONTEST
OUTWALKED A HORSE
REINBOLD DEFEATED A TENNESSEE WALKING HORSE BY 12 MINUTES

Baseball's all-time "hit parade" occurred on July 10, 1932, in an 18-inning game between the Indians and the Athletics. The two teams banged out a total of 58 hits. The final score was 18-17, Indians, and the winning pitcher was Ed Rommel who allowed—get this—29 hits!

A TRIPLE DEAD HEAT

WAS RE-RUN IN NEW SOUTH WALES, AUSTRALIA
AND ENDED IN

ANOTHER TRIPLE DEAD HEAT

THE HORSES WERE
"HIGH FLYER" - "LOCH LOCHIE" AND "BARDINI"

Moorefield, Sydney - Oct. 10, 1903

MRS. CHRISTIAN ALMER
of Grindelwald, Switzerland
WHO HAD NEVER BEFORE CLIMBED A MOUNTAIN
CELEBRATED HER 50TH WEDDING ANNIVERSARY
WITH HER 70-YEAR-OLD HUSBAND-A VETERAN GUIDE-
BY ASCENDING THE 12,150-FOOT WETTERHORN!

Before the aluminum and then the fiberglass pole made 16 and 17 feet vaults commonplace, a pole vaulter named Cornelius Warmerdam dominated the event like it had never been dominated before or since. He was the first vaulter to clear 15 feet with a bamboo pole—and he did it 43 times before anyone else could achieve that height.

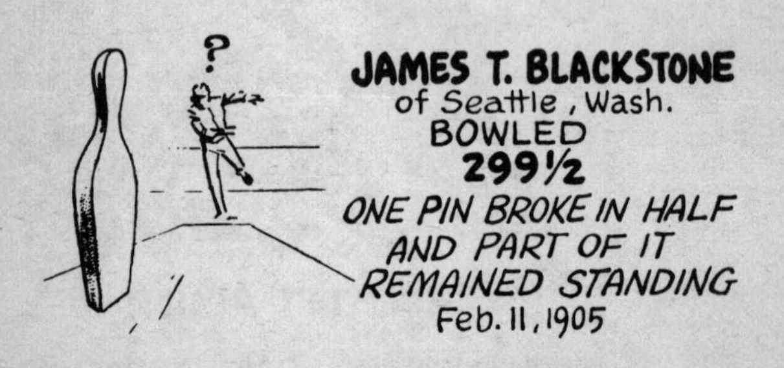

Penn State College didn't lose a soccer game for eight straight years. They won 65 and tied 5 between 1933 and 1940.

STEFAN STEINBERGER
WITHOUT ONCE PAUSING TO REST WALKED FROM HIS HOME IN BAVARIA TO ST. GILGEN, AUSTRIA– A DISTANCE OF 42 MILES– AND THEN CLIMBED THE SCHAFBERG MOUNTAIN 5,900 FEET HIGH!

BURLEIGH GRIMES

Brooklyn 1925

HIT INTO 2 DOUBLE PLAYS
AND ONE TRIPLE PLAY IN SUCCESSION

E. COOK - Oklahoma University halfback - **SWAM TO A TOUCHDOWN!**
A BLOCKED KICK FELL INTO A RIVER BEHIND THE GOAL POSTS AND COOK SWAM THE BALL BACK FOR A TOUCHDOWN (Guthrie, Okla. - Nov. 6, 1904)

No one ever had to tell Christy Mathewson to exercise control. During the 1918 season the Giants' immortal hurled 68 consecutive innings without walking a man. P.S.: For 12 seasons in a row, Matty won 20 or more games; for three straight seasons he won 30 or more; and in the 1905 World Series he pitched three shut-outs.

DELIVERY BOYS
in Tokyo, Japan,
RIDE THROUGH BUSY STREETS ON BICYCLES
BALANCING WITH ONE HAND 20 OR MORE BOXED ORDERS OF NOODLES

MAROTTE BEAUPRÉ
A FRENCH ACTRESS FOUGHT A RAPIER DUEL IN 1669 ON THE STAGE BEFORE AN AUDIENCE OF SEVERAL HUNDRED PEOPLE WHO THOUGHT THEY WERE WITNESSING A SCENE FROM THE PLAY
-UNTIL MAROTTE'S OPPONENT, CATHERINE DE URLIS, FELL SERIOUSLY WOUNDED

"OLD HOSS"
RADBOURNE –
PITCHED AND WON 9 GAMES
IN 10 DAYS.

Providence, 1884.

Fans who enjoy watching horsehides flying over fences got their money's worth on July 10, 1929, in a game between the Pirates and the Phillies. One home run—no more, no less—was hit in each inning.

THE STRANGEST HANDICAP RACE IN HISTORY!

KILBURN HOYT of Dunbarton, N.H.,
GIVEN A **500**-FOOT HEAD START
IN A **1,000**-FOOT RACE, DEFEATED
HAMLET PERKINS OF NEARBY HOPKINTON
ALTHOUGH HOYT RAN WITH A 225-LB. MAN ON HIS SHOULDERS! (July 4, 1826)

DR. VICTOR REINDERS
of Waukesha, Wis.,
FIRING AT A TOTAL OF **122,700**
CLAY PIGEONS IN TOURNAMENTS
BROKE 120,317 OF THEM, FOR A SCORING RECORD OF 98.0578 %
USING THE SAME 12-GAUGE SHOTGUN, HE HAS FIRED A TOTAL OF **436,000** SHELLS
-REPRESENTING 15⅓ TONS OF SHOT

GUNNAR ERIKSEN
of Fauske, Norway,
SKIED FROM FAUSKE TO VALDRES
- A DISTANCE OF **806** MILES -
ALTHOUGH HE IS TOTALLY BLIND!
Feb. 13 To April 14, 1966

JIM
LONDOS
FORMER
WORLD'S WRESTLING
CHAMPION
RAN A MILE
WITH 2 MEN
ON HIS BACK

GREATEST
GRIDIRON
PERFORMANCE!
Red Grange
Illinois vs. Michigan, 1924,
HANDLED THE BALL 5 TIMES-
SCORED 5 TOUCHDOWNS!
HIS RUNS WERE 95-67-56-45-15 YARDS

"BROKER'S TIP"
Owned by Colonel E. R. BRADLEY
WON ONLY ONE RACE IN HIS LIFE
THE KENTUCKY DERBY–1933
PAYING **$49,600**
IT WAS HIS ***FIRST*** *VICTORY AND HIS* ***LAST!***

THE MOST AMAZING MARKSMEN IN THE WORLD!

RIFLEMEN COMPETING IN A STRANGE CONTEST AT TAMWEG, AUSTRIA, SHOOT AT TARGETS LOCATED 426 FEET ACROSS LAKE PREBER - AND MUST AIM AT THEIR TARGET'S REFLECTION IN THE WATER!
THE COMPETITION HAS BEEN HELD SINCE 1834 AND THE REFLECTION IS 160 FEET DISTANT FROM THE TARGET ***-YET IN 21 MATCHES COMPETITORS RICOCHETED BULLETS OFF THE WATER AND HIT A 7-INCH BULL'S-EYE DEAD CENTER!***

SAM
CHAPMAN
Philadelphia
Athletics
HIT 2 HOME RUNS
IN 2 DAYS
IN THE SAME
GAME
IN ONE GAME HE
HIT ONE HOMER
BEFORE MIDNIGHT
AND THE SECOND
AFTER MIDNIGHT
July 30-31,
1941

C.G. WILSON
of St. Joseph, Mo.,
AIMING BY MEANS OF
A MIRROR,
SHOOTS A CROSSBOW OVER
HIS SHOULDER, HITS THE
TRIGGER OF ANOTHER
CROSSBOW BEHIND HIM, AND
THAT WEAPON SHOOTS AN APPLE OFF HIS OWN HEAD

CHARLES McCOY - of FORT WORTH, Texas
MADE 31 ERRORS IN ONE GAME 1932

NICKY TIRONE
AGE 2
Brooklyn, N.Y.
HIT A BASEBALL OVER A TWO-STORY BUILDING

JAMES
HINSON
of Monroe, N C
MADE
16 HITS
IN SUCCESSION
AS A
PINCH-HITTER
1923

STANLEY HAWKINS

Center Fielder, Mountain View, Calif

WAS AT BAT **4** TIMES, April 22, 1928
HIT SAFELY **4** TIMES
SCORED **4** RUNS
STOLE **4** BASES
CAUGHT **4** FLIES
BATTED **444** FOR SEASON
OF **44** GAMES

The University of Minnesota football team rolled up 725 points in 13 games in 1904—averaging 55.7 points to their opponents' 0.9 per game.

BILLY HERMAN
(Second Baseman of the Cubs)

PLAYING HIS *FIRST* YEAR IN THE LEAGUE IN HIS *FIRST* WORLD SERIES WAS *FIRST* MAN UP IN THE *FIRST* INNING OF THE *FIRST* GAME AND SCORED THE *FIRST* HIT AND THE *FIRST* RUN He also made the LAST HIT and the LAST RUN in the LAST inning of the LAST game

LOUIS CYR
(1863-1912)
WHO WEIGHED 340 POUNDS
AND WAS KNOWN AS
THE CANADIAN HERCULES,
SUPPORTED HIS 125-POUND WIFE
AS SHE CLIMBED A LADDER
-WHICH HE HELD IN ONE
OUTSTRETCHED HAND

Between 1959 and 1965, Tommy Davis of the 49ers attempted 234 points after touchdown—and didn't miss one.

HOWARD HILL FAMED AMERICAN ARCHER
ARMED ONLY WITH A CONVENTIONAL BOW
KILLED A 12-FOOT THRESHER SHARK WITH A SINGLE ARROW
WHILE UNDER WATER AT A DEPTH OF 40 FEET

THE SHARK WAS ONLY 15 FEET AWAY BUT HILL MASTERED HITTING A TARGET UNDER WATER AT A DISTANCE OF 60 FEET

The greatest "stealer" of all time had to be Ty Cobb. He stole 892 bases during his career, and on three occasions he reached first and then proceeded to steal second, third, and home.

WILLIAM WILLIS
SAILED 6,700 MILES FROM PERU TO SAMOA IN **112** DAYS ON A RAFT CONSISTING OF **7** BALSA LOGS LASHED TOGETHER
AT THE AGE OF 61
HIS ONLY COMPANIONS WERE A CAT AND A PARROT–
AND THE CAT ATE THE PARROT (1954)

"SNOOKS"
DOWD
of Lehigh
RAN 210 YARDS
TO A TOUCHDOWN!
HE RAN THE
WRONG
DIRECTION
CIRCLED AROUND
HIS OWN GOAL POSTS
AND RAN BACK AGAIN!

ANNE FELTS
of the Ashland City
(Tenn.) Cubs
IN A
BASKETBALL
GAME AGAINST
CHARLOTTE
(Tenn.) H.S.
SCORED EVERY
POINT MADE
BY HER TEAM
- WINNING
31 TO 29

HERB PRUETT
Pitching for St. Louis
FANNED 'BABE RUTH
13 OUT OF 15 TIMES
1923

SOUTHMONT H.S. DEFEATED DALE H.S. IN A FOOTBALL GAME **33 TO 27**
-WITHOUT MAKING A SINGLE FIRST DOWN
Johnstown Pa.-Oct. 28, 1952